THIS BOOK BELONGS TO

Vicky Rasinske

PUBLISHED IN 2020 BY VICKY RASINSKE

COLOR TEST

Basic tips of Drawing!

- ★ A little bit of art theory is always good to know, Lets start........
- ★ All you need is a pencil,eraser and a piece off paper!
- ★ Draw lightly at first because you might need to erase some lines as you work.
- ★ Add details according to the diagrams but dont worry about being perfect. Artists frequently make mistakes they just find ways to make their mistakes look interesting.
- ★ Dont worry if your drawing dont turn out the way you want them to , just keep practicing ! Sometimes drawing the same thing just a few times will help.
- ★ Once you have finished your drawing in pencil you can trace it with a black fineliner pen and color or paint it to your liking.

Turn the page for some cool composition ideas!!!

SQUAD
315
S: 315

ARMY
15 Km

TANK
DIV.
TRAINING
CAMP

JUNIOR
ARMY
JUNIOR

JUNIOR
SQUAD
BH ON4 RD

Have any questions?

We want to hear from you!

Just Scan

Please consider writing a review!

THANK
YOU

www.ingramcontent.com/pod-product-compliance
Lightning Source LLC
Chambersburg PA
CBHW081239250726
48654CB00012B/1402
* 9 7 9 8 7 0 5 8 4 7 8 7 7 *